THE LONELINESS PARADOX

HASHEM, HUMANITY, HEALTHINESS, HAPPINESS, AND HOPE

BY

GAIL HELENE BRETAN, PH.D.

RABBI HARRY Z. SKY, D.D.

WITH

CAROL RAUCH, M.A.

Quiet Waters Publications

Bolivar, Missouri

2014

Quiet Waters Publications
P.O. Box 34, Bolivar, MO 65613-0034

www.quietwaterspub.com

Cover Design: Elisabeth Dreher,
                   Cynthia Johnson

ISBN 978-1-931475-61-7
Library of Congress Control Number: 2014909264

The Loneliness Paradox

Hashem, Humanity, Healthiness, Happiness, and Hope

To our extended families,
including you, dear reader,
we feel connected,
driving out the loneliness.

TABLE OF CONTENTS

We are all
so much together,
but we are all
dying of loneliness.

– ALBERT SCHWEITZER

INTRODUCTION

In terms of loneliness, the theme of this book, we have seen so much of it, and of the suffering caused by loneliness, that we felt compelled to address it and write about it.

We believe there is too much loneliness in our world, and we seek to discuss its process as well as its Jewish perspectives. We hope to help people make connections to their Jewishness and to one another through this project.

We are an odd pair, or unusual triumvirate, if you consider all of us involved in the writing and editing of this treatise.

Rabbi Dr. Harry Sky brings ninety years of questioning the status quo, of challenging the system, and of being moved by passionate feelings of justice for all. All of this finds expression in his nightly dreams.

Dr. Gail Bretan, Ph. D., brings fifty-seven years of facilitating trans-denominational networks, of providing ideas and resources to better serve our communities, and of being moved by compassionate connections.

Carol Rauch, M.A., brings the silent passion of the magical cat, of playing the harp, and of being moved by nuances in words and actions.

Each one of us brings observed and experienced perspectives to this *Loneliness Paradox*. You may notice three voices in these pages, creating a dialogue we invite you to join.

Whenever possible, we try to identify the "I" of each speaker – as our voices are woven into each other throughout the text of this book.

We also bring our Judaism to this issue, which is the foundation that offers a remedy to this plague of *Loneliness*.

In this book, we will be using the terms *elderly, senior, older person, mature adult*, etc., interchangeably. In addition, we will be using many words that might not be part of your vocabulary, such as Hebrew or Yiddish words. You can generally find these words written in *italics*, and most are listed in the Glossary section at the end of this book. These references are to help you understand.

It is written in the Bible that "you should rise before the elderly and honor the aged" (Leviticus 19:32). The Hebrew word for elderly – *zaken* – is an acronym for *zeh shkaneh hakhma*, which literally translates as *a person who has acquired wisdom*. We, the authors, being people of advanced age, advanced degrees, and advanced experiences, will occasionally refer to ourselves and to you as *zaken* – in wisdom and in love.

Background to
the Loneliness Paradox

We are writing this book because we are particularly troubled by the loneliness epidemic we are witnessing in society, especially among the elderly. In this book, we will be using stories, Jewish concepts, personal and communal experiences, and our personal philosophies as a springboard to discuss the problems of and possible solutions for the loneliness puzzle. We are encouraging a "Jewish dialectic" (which is the title of Harry's third book) – with you as our partner.

A *dialectic* is a reasoning which uses dialogue as a method of intellectual investigation. A *dialectic* can also be the nature of logical argumentation, or it can be the juxtaposition or interaction of conflicting ideas and perceptions. However, loneliness, as we know, is not always treated as an intellectual subject – it is often emotional or even spiritual. This book explores these realms and brings them together – connecting heart, mind, and soul.

We will begin with an intellectual underpinning of the *concept* of loneliness and from there move on to the emotional, the physical, the social, and especially the spiritual aspects of loneliness. At times, all these parts will converge comprising a greater whole.

Loneliness begins with the value or –may actually be intensified by– the *lack* of value (devaluation) attributed to mature or older adults – the *zaken* – in our communities and in our lives.

This devaluation is formed and perpetuated by both, society and our own selves. Our cultural and social norms create these devaluations. These devaluations include:

- the devaluation of mature age (sometimes referred to as *old* age) – because of the societal emphasis on youth
- the devaluation of the experience that leads to wisdom – because of the emphasis placed on facts but not on the analyses and syntheses of these facts
- the devaluation of education for mature adults – because of the emphasis on acquiring *useful knowledge*, such as for job-skills in careers (which are not seen as needed in retirement)
- the devaluation of lifelong learning activities – because of expecting a decline in mental faculties and memory
- the devaluation of personal meaning – because of the emphasis placed on mass consumption, peer pressure, and external or impersonal meaning
- the devaluation of community connections – because of the emphasis placed on individual autonomy and ambition
- the devaluation of critical thinking, reflection, and action – because of the emphasis placed on accepting old belief systems
- the devaluation of religious, spiritual, and moral principles – because of the emphasis placed on principals of science and rationality

This means that we hold individual values that appear to be in stark contrast with our collective communal values and responsibilities.

Within this contrast, we hold a *duality* about maturity. On the one hand, we are taught to respect our elders and the wisdom they have attained throughout their lives.

On the other hand, our society is obsessed with youth, as expressed in our media and corporate representations. Grey hairs are dyed, faces are surgically lifted, true age is secretly guarded, birthdays remind us that we are *over the hill*, and occasional lapses in memory or judgment are explained away as *senior moments* to be feared and avoided. *OLD* becomes synonymous with *decrepit, falling apart,* and *useless*.

The view that retirement is a time for consigning senior citizens to the rocking-chair on the porch and for pushing mature individuals from their jobs to make way for *new and bold ideas* is simply mistaken. While the term *active senior* is often regarded oxymoronically, *active* and *senior* are not mutually exclusive.

Even from a religious perspective, which accords the *divine spark* to reside within every individual, such devaluation of an *elder* as *inactive* is immoral for stereotyping and condemning an entire population.

Individuals of the aging populace should not be obstructed from reaching their earthly as well as sacred potentials. Even secular humanism views such devaluation, that of wasting human potential, as equally immoral.

In other words, the problem of ageism is not just a corporeal (physical) problem (*spacing* or placing people in nursing homes); it is a reasoning and moral problem as well, since it creates spaces and places for older people to eliminate them from our thoughts and conscious levels (Bretan, 2013).

The attributes *old* and *ignorable,* continually applied to older and mature people, are completely inaccurate as proven persuasively by mounting evidence to the contrary. Sadler (2006) claims that retirement is a relatively new institution. Previous generations could not afford to retire, or they did not live long enough to do so. Institutionalizing retirement in the 20th century was seen as a fitting finish to a working life at a time when the average life expectancy still was about 65 years.

However, this concept of retirement is in keeping neither with the nature of work in the information-age nor with the increase of human longevity. Therefore, this period is marked by the term, "Third Age" (Sadler, 2006, p. 15).

The moral imperative of valuing maturity is reflected in the continuous research emerging from studies of individuals entering the so-called *Third Age* or being in their *third stage* of life. Accordingly, older people should be perceived as sound human beings who still have much to offer the society.

Research demonstrates convincingly how people of the Baby Boomer generation –born between 1946 and 1964– seek to remain active, provide meaningful service to the community (*giving back*), and thereby attain personal self-fulfillment.

In 2004, researchers at the Harvard School of Public Health along with the Met Life Foundation Initiative on Retirement and Civic Engagement found that older adults rely on the quality of social connectedness because that is

> where the real promise of improving the quality of community life lies, played out through a variety of mechanisms, formal and informal, structured and unstructured, organized and unorganized. (Sadler, 2006, p. 15)

This book also addresses the devaluation not only of civic engagement but also of compassion for others, especially the lack of compassion for elders, culminating in the rampant abuse of elders. All these devaluations affect our moral compasses and practices. Since we are Jews, we will look at these issues from an action-oriented Jewish point of view, one that is rooted in social justice. This perspective, as well, is often devalued, disregarded, disparaged, and even denigrated by non-Jewish communities.

Loneliness is a type of prison (Foucault, 1975); it can affect and limit one's physical, emotional, social, intellectual, and spiritual freedom and growth. We are reminded of the liturgy of "Min HaMeetzar Karati" – *From my prison I called to Hashem, The Holy One.* Hashem answered us – and we were transported from an enclosed and restrictive place to an open and liberating space.

We believe that older people still have much to offer not only to society, but also to each other, and especially to themselves. The elderly should not be confined to this *prison* of Loneliness, they should be enabled to continue sharing their skills, their experience, and their wisdom as vital benefactors!

In the introduction, we have explored concepts and experiences of loneliness as well as the suffering it causes. We view it a moral imperative to act on this information. The first chapter will offer perspectives on loneliness from within Jewish contexts.

And the Lord God said,
It is not good that
the man should be alone;
I will make him a fitting
helper.

– GENESIS 2:18

Chapter 1

LONELINESS – A JEWISH QUESTION

When we consider the problems of our later years, we are always accompanied by conscious and subconscious memories and feelings of years gone by. Our earliest memories are sometimes key to opening the doors of our souls, our psyches. In Jewish tradition the *soul / neshama / breath* is a gift from the Creator of all life. Each one of us, from the moment of birth to the end of our natural life, is embarking upon a journey. The roadmap, like all maps, keeps on adjusting and readjusting. It is impossible to say, at any time, the map that I know is the final map of my life.

Some authorities, when speaking of this map, use the Hebrew word, *halacha* (*halakha*), which means *journey*. A person who knows him or herself as a Jew, guided by his or her map, may experience modifications during his or her life. Some of us who feel guided by this map believe that being Jewish involves meeting the following requirements:

First, an active agent, better known as the *Creator* or *God*, presented us with a map for our lives. No matter what you may or may not be doing, Jews will label that you are *bashert* – you are *being destined*. Instead of *bashert*, some will call it your *mazel*.

The word *mazel* means *constellation*. When our ancestors lived in Babylon, they encountered Zoroastrians, and accepted their beliefs. In Jewish scriptures, the glory of *El* (God) is told in the heavens. And how can we know the messages of the heavens? Through reading the *mazalot,* the *constellation* of the stars. These *mazelot* will provide the direction of your personal life.

Assuming this to be true and correct, are we then still left with free will? Are we responsible for anything that happens to us? Can we choose? Do we have the freedom to say *yes* and *no* about things and events? The Jewish sages say, *yes,* for there is *hashem.* God has power over the *mazalot*; and if you turn to *hashem,* God will respond and free you from the clutches of the *mazalot.* Part of being Jewish is acknowledging that *hashem* is the God above all gods.

Secondly, the word we translate as *journey* has been known for centuries as an *eternal code.* We have the tradition of the Ten Commandments given to us at Mt. Sinai. Observing these commandments as well as the many traditional rules and regulations (613 of them) has been considered the Jewish norm until recent times

Since the time of Napoleon, various groups have sprung up within the Jewish ethos and culture focusing on one part of the traditional *halacha* or another. Many claimed that it is impossible to live by the 613 commandments. Some make sense, others do not; some apply to our times, others do not; some are sexist, others are not; some are discriminatory, others are egalitarian. You can always stir the pot, bring something to the surface by saying, "That's it! That part makes me a Jew. The rest I choose not to observe."

Our tradition cannot make up its mind. There has never been a moment in Jewish history when every single Jew belonged to only one party. Some live within certain boundaries. Others live without boundaries while still claiming their right of being considered Jews.

A recognized value in Judaism is the ability to interpret Biblical texts through contemporary as well as historical prisms. These prisms unite the needs of the collective and individual perspectives with traditional as well as new meanings. Berlin and Brettler (Jewish Publication Society, 2004) elaborate as follows:

> The tradition of Biblical interpretation has been a constant conversation, at times an argument, among its participants; at no period has the text been interpreted in a monolithic fashion. If anything marks Jewish biblical interpretation it is the diversity of approaches employed and the multiplicity of meanings produced. (p. ix)

Berlin and Brettler also add that just as there is no one Jewish interpretation, "there is no authorized Jewish translation of the Bible into English" (p. x) or into any other language. That is why "each generation must, as it were, stand again at Sinai finding new layers of significant and understanding in the text" (Shapiro, 1999, p. 13). Consequently, personal and communal interpretations of Judaism differ.

Jews in their senior years will review their lives and prepare to leave it, they will cling to their belief and program of Jewishness. To each one of them we say, "Don't worry about the rest of the Jewish world. You made the choice for yourself." That to us is the ultimate answer. If you can accept yourself and live by that acceptance, then the rest of the world is of very little consequence.

The only thing to remember, no matter what group you belong to, no matter what definition of *halacha* you assume, is that Jewishness is whatever assures life. Whoever judges and chooses, whoever includes some and excludes others, is not one of us. We do not ever say, "for this you go to heaven, for that you go to hell." We do speak of "a world to come" in which every soul will return to the all-soul from which it has been separated.

This philosophical explanation and exercise was placed here to help one understand that there is always choice within Judaism, as there is within life. Seen through this Jewish prism, even loneliness can be considered a personal choice.

And what about a communal choice?

In this chapter, we explored the idea of loneliness through Jewish *halakha*, interpretations, and personal choices. In the next chapter, we will look at communal concerns.

The eternal quest of
the individual human being
is to shatter his loneliness.

– Norman Cousins

Chapter II

THE VALUE OF COMMUNAL CONNECTION

As Jews, we do not overcome our loneliness by the *love concept*. For us, we overcome it by our sense of connectedness to God, to nature, and to one another. Judaism is a communal religion. When we pray together, such as on *Yom Kippur*, we do not say, "*I sinned.*" We say, "*We sinned,*" so as not to point the finger or single out anyone. When we mourn, such as during *shiva*, we do it as a community.

Our tradition teaches us that, at the moment of creation, the Creator brought to life one human being. We are all descendants of that one. In Scripture, we read, "It is not good for *the human* to be alone." God spoke these words to the Universe, and therefore, went about creating a companion. The companion is part of the initial creation process.

When people talk about finding their soul mates, many feel that this is the connection to the lost part of self. On a broader scale, since we are all part of the same family, we all have pieces that connect us to one another.

Recent scientific studies focusing on our cellular levels through DNA[1] have discovered our mitochon-

---

[1] www.pbs.org/wgbh/nova/neanderthals/mtdna.html

drial ancestors. These studies show that the human cell, whether it be male or female, contains within itself the past and anticipates the future, which supports our perspective on the oneness of humankind. In our rapidly changing society, we are so occupied with our own lives that we forget to connect to others. Our connection to all life is inherent in our DNA. For instance, every cell in the male line appears to have a bundle as its tale. All examined cells have that bundle. Variations occur in the extended part of the cell while the base indicates the commonness.

Beyond the base, we have lessons of variation. Therefore, no major differences exist based on physical variations. Neither the pigment of the skin, nor the structure of your spine decides who you are. Everything is registered in the spaces of our brain. Everything is referenced in our individual cells.

Although physical evidence already proves our connectedness, we also believe in exploring its social dimensions. According to research of social sciences, communal focus yields greater longevity and happiness.

We, the writers, have just shared a package of figs, ruminating the many analogies and various imagery of the mighty fig. A single fig, full of natural sweetness, contains many seeds that are comparable to a healthy, functioning community. Adam and Eve covered their nakedness with a fig leaf, which suggests the eternal truth that all of us have a seed from the same plant. The fig leaf is a symbol of oneness. Once

Adam and Eve discovered their physical uniqueness, they covered themselves with a fig leaf, which represented total oneness of all nature.

We must address the human community in such terms, since we assume that we are all descendants from the same seed, and that each one of us is a carrier of the complete experience of the initial seed. All of us, therefore, carry within the same inclinations which make all of us human.

In the Book of Genesis, the first book of the Hebrew Bible, the first human is called, *Adam*, which means *red earth*. The translators of the Hebrew Bible sometimes lose sight of this. *Adam* literally means *red*. In the Middle East, the color red seems to have a special significance, often used as a symbol of insecurity. One never knows, according to folklore, what a red-head may bring into a situation.

From the Biblical story, we arrive at the notion that even the uncertainty, the doubtfulness, the tenuousness must be considered in every human situation; therefore, an individual who is limited physically or tainted by *redness* is not to be discarded. This individual, too, is part of creation.

Red is also a symbol of blood. When we speak of our family, we talk about our blood relatives or our bloodline. In the creation story, we can trace our bloodline to the first cell, again talking about the connectedness of humanity. The term, *humanity*, has been clichéd and taken on many meanings, often losing its initial nuance.

According to the dictionary, *humanity* has come to mean many of the following words or phrases:

- compassion
- brotherly love
- fraternity
- fellow feeling
- philanthropy
- humaneness
- kindness
- consideration
- understanding
- sympathy
- tolerance
- leniency
- mercy
- mercifulness
- clemency
- pity
- tenderness
- benevolence
- charity
- goodness
- magnanimity
- generosity

… and we are sure you can come up with a few more synonyms.

Most of these concepts will be woven throughout this document, but right now we want to talk about the innate aspects of *humanity*, indeed, of *humanness*. In Judaism, we have the concepts of *yetzer harah* – questionable inclinations – and *yetzer hatov* – worthy inclinations. A second assumption in Jewish thinking is that one should attempt to compromise one's differences. The person with the questionable inclination has within him/herself the capacity for worthy inclinations.

On the other hand, the opposite is true. Many people with worthy inclinations also contain within themselves questionable inclinations. The great Hasidic teacher, Shneor Zalman of Ladi, urged his followers to pursue the middle way. One is never totally good; nor is one ever totally evil. The human journey sets us on the path of conciliation between the two.

Take generosity and selfishness for example. I may be generous with my immediate family but dismiss communal needs. I may be community-minded, but my family is lacking for much. A parent who is forever homebound and completely oblivious to the world around him or her is suffering from one-sidedness. The parent who is forever attending meetings and seldom ever finding time for his offspring is suffering from blindness.

In our senior years, we tend to review our past lives. Sometimes this brings feelings of guilt, of missed chances, of blindness to possibilities. When we are unable to face these situations directly, we often fall into asocial patterns of behavior, giving us that *cocoon*-feeling and providing us with a strange sense of comfort.

Picture yourself being inside a cylinder. It turns round and round, and you, the occupant of the cylinder, initiate the rotation of the cylinder. You go round and round, you never come to any conclusion, and you always wonder where you might be headed, asking continually, *"Where am I going?"*

The senior years are a time of development, not of cessation. Yet, we would like to bring everything to rest. We would like a calm existence. Our faces seem drawn and a blank mask covers them. We cling to this pattern. It is easier that way. We do not have to ask questions. We do not have to wonder, *"Why did I do this? Why did I not do that?"*

The great task of the senior years is to let go of the loneliness and to find within oneself the evolved person we have become. We have had many significant moments in our lives. Some of us got married, some of us did not. Some of us chose a same-sex marriage as a pattern of life, some of us did not. Some of us bore children, some of us did not. Some of us generated new ideas, some of us realized never known meanings in sacred texts, and so forth and so on.

What we are suggesting is that the senior years can become the statement of fulfillment, the statement of closure we seem to need in our human endeavors.

One day while visiting Israel, I (Harry) met an elderly person. He was carrying a volume of the Talmud, and I, in a friendly fashion, asked him, "What are you studying?" He answered, "The chapter on returning lost property." And then he said, "One must be sure to study every day, for it is written if you neglect your studies one day, you have lost two."

For many years, I have not understood this statement. What would be so terrible about not studying one day? So what if you do not continue your human search every single day? The Easterners teach us that each day has an existence of its own. They say, "Live the day. Learn how to focus. Respect the moment. You have an opportunity to take a sacred text and use it as a guide in the world in which you live. You did not avail yourself of the opportunity." Perhaps in that moment, if you had availed yourself of its energy, you could have resolved a deep and trying problem. And instead of sadness, happiness would have prevailed as part of your day.

I know from my own experience that the days in which I have a study-partner are my most gratifying ones. I have one partner with whom I study *Mussar* (Jewish ethical living), another with whom I study *Talmud*, and a third with whom I study the implications of events in the world. I feel better when my mind works that way. I feel sated when I think that way. I feel I have partially discovered the purpose of my life.

Studying is one way to relieve our loneliness, to leave it behind for a moment.

You might ask, "What is study?" In Jewish tradition, study is the cure-all for everything that troubles you: If you have a headache, study! If you are fearful, study! If you don't know where you are headed in life, take out a book and read.

When I (Harry) was young, I had another remedy for loneliness, or whenever finding myself with *nothing to do*. It was fantasy. I cannot possibly number the times when I would wash away the negative and dark thoughts inside of me with a tale that came to my mind, sometimes true, sometimes fantasy. I suppose that was another form of study, for what is study if not probing and testing old stories and old traditions.

I began to separate fact from fiction in my life when I was approximately thirty years old. I had been ordained as rabbi in 1951. I was 27-years-old and, for the first time, I faced reality as it spread out in front of me. It was hard. It was difficult. In my first congregation, I became deeply involved in the arts scene, even being cited in the town's newspaper for my contributions. That was my stage, the place where I could tell stories, real or made-up, and live life as I knew it.

I remember my first encounter with congregational reality. The sisterhood had planned a congregational supper and, lo and behold, the food-dishes were mixed, the *kashrut* rules had not been applied. My vice president said to me that we were a non-orthodox congregation. That is why we turned to the seminary for a rabbi who would believe that the old ways would not be the only ways. I started to walk away, and one of the officers stopped me and tried to pacify the situation.

About a month or two later, my wife and I went to Boston and bought kosher meat. We had a wonderful roast and invited the vice president for *Shabbat* dinner. We served the roast, and he said, "I thought you kept kosher." I said I do. "Where did you get such good meat?" he inquired. "In Boston," I replied. We had a so-called kosher butcher in town, but since his customers were few, his produce was not the best. If you wanted fresher kosher food, you went to Boston.

This vice president felt that I was on trial and refused to give me a long-term contract, which led to a decade of search. Where would I really find my own soul? Ultimately, the answer was Portland, Maine, in 1961. I still continue to serve there as a rabbi for the high holidays. These early struggles and episodes of loneliness ultimately led me to a congregation of a lifetime, literally. These struggles and isolations did not define me or limit me.

Assuming I am correct when I say that loneliness is part of the human condition, it would fit the mystical and Hassidic notions of Judaism. Loneliness is, in their terms, the *sitra achra – the other way*, not the way that leads to fulfillment and closeness to God, but rather to separation and to the constant feeling of aloneness in this world. There are many people for whom this is their *modus operandi*. Soren Kierkegaard addressed this *aloneness* as did Franz Kafka.

In keeping with the communal theme of this chapter, we invite you to consider practicing the Jewish concept of *Hahnasat Orhim* (literally, *welcoming guests*, or the *act of hospitality*), as highlighted by Jonathan Sacks (2005):

> Jewish ethics is refreshingly down-to-earth. If someone is in need, give. If someone is lonely, invite them home. If someone you know has recently been bereaved, visit them and give them comfort. If you know of someone who has lost their

job, do all you can to help them find another. The
sages called this 'imitating God'. They went further: giving hospitality to a stranger, they said, is
even greater than receiving the divine presence.
This is a religion at its most humanizing and hu-
mane. So too is the insistence that the ethical life
is a form of celebration. Doing good is not pain-
ful, a matter of our duty and a chastising conscious." (p. 5)

What Rabbi Sacks is elucidating is that in serving
others, we emulate God, and at the same time, we re-
discover our humanness. It is through these connections – to God and to others – that our loneliness is
transmuted, if only for a short while. With continued
practice, loneliness is transmuted and sometimes
transformed for long periods of time.

At times, loneliness is part of all human experience.
It is part of the cycle of life. And communal connection is a practice that can also relieve loneliness.

In this chapter, we viewed the value of connections
– to God and to others – that have the power to
transmute our loneliness. The next chapter will further transmute loneliness by exploring and experiencing various states of clarity.

The older generation had
greater respect for land than
for science. But we live in an
age when science, more than
soil, has become the provider
of growth and abundance.
Living just on the land
creates loneliness
in an age of globalism.

– SHIMON PERES

Chapter III

Loneliness as a State of Clarity

Every so often, we encounter a wonderful painting. The subject usually is the awesomeness of nature. We see ourselves standing on a mountain peak, softly caressing winds blowing around us. We hear a sweet, soft sound, and we know that all is well in the world. We are convinced that nature is an ally rather than a foe. As humans, we feel called upon to testify before the entire world that there is a goodness in this world. We can find it. We can own it.

Today, many people are expressing great concern about our environment. The smokestacks spewing out their compounded doses of carbon monoxide, the riverbeds overflowing with human detritus, our books overflowing with statements of pain and suffering. Or, as my Yiddish-speaking relatives would say, *Oy vay!*

As Jews, we cannot in all good conscience accept this negativity and simply say that this is the way the world was, is, and will be. We insist that change is possible. And change for the better being preferable.

What is change? For some people, change is a variation of *what is*. For others, change is an evolving *what is* into something beyond the current *what is*. Throughout life, we are caught between those two poles. One pole says that change is an act of becoming; the other says that change is a reformulation of the established. Each of us makes that choice in life. An older person who has recently been told by his/her physician that much is happening to his/her body may say, "I'm on a slippery slope, not heading upwards but downwards, landing who knows where." Another person may say, "Okay. I've reached this point. It's a high point. It's higher than what was before. I'm older. I know more. I'm more experienced. I have a broader perspective than others who may be as old as I am or younger."

The choice is yours: are you going to be stationary? or will you remain in a constant state of becoming?

Throughout our lives we ask the question, *Who am I?* or *What am I?* Sometimes we find satisfactory answers. At other times we see ourselves dangling, going from here to there and backwards. In the theologies of many traditions, you have aspects of the leading deity that seem to be of a stationary nature and other aspects as parts of an evolving nature. Someone once said it depends on the train on which you plan to take your journey. The choice is yours.

We, therefore, suggest that we of the senior community pay attention to this issue. We even venture to say that if you can find your place in the *state of constantly becoming*, your life will feel fuller and less open to the fixations of loneliness.

I (Harry) have always pictured myself on a never-ending journey. From that point of view, with an open heart and with open eyes as prerequisite, I have been presented with an extraordinary way of life. Do not criticize; just suggest. There is no one standing on a platform haranguing me, there is only conversation.

During the past few weeks, I sensed in myself a turbulence in need of being addressed. My political philosophy has always been that all humankind is really one race. It is true that in various parts of the world, political leaders and others attempt to label and distinguish various groups, awarding greater value to some over others. This sort of turbulence is not new in my life. My ultimate goal, however, is to further the concept of *oneness*.

I will never forget one of my earliest memories. I was sitting in a one-room bookstore with some balloons in one hand while tearing pages from a Hebrew book with the other. None of the pages were harmed. They remained intact. It seems after much analysis my intent was not to discard the pages of the book, but rather to change their order. There was a voice in that room that sought to arrest my behavior, but in my stubbornness, I continued to tear the pages from the book.

I learned a lesson from that image. We are often, unknowingly, in a process of reshaping and reordering our existence. As a Jew, I could never refuse this exercise. Change in Jewish life is central. Our traditions have always changed from generation to generation. Perhaps one of the prescriptions we would offer for loneliness is to acquaint ourselves with the old practice called, *CHANGE*.

Oft times we have conversations with people who are facing the retirement years (65 plus). They are tired of their current life, they feel as if the spark is gone, and at times they wonder, "What am I achieving by what I'm doing?" Sometimes, when we hear such comments, we are reminded of vehicles in need of refueling or perhaps in need of readjusting.

The point we want to make is that retirement is more than a matter of years. Why should I retire if I can still think and shape and affect? When we are involved in such a conversation, I sometimes feel the answer lies in the question posed. Feeling useless or seeing oneself as lacking creative juices, potential retirees cannot see their possibilities. Sometimes, by standing in the forest, one does not see the beautiful tree right there.

From the moment of our conception, there lies within us a light, a direction, a yearning waiting to be fulfilled. No matter how successful our lives may be, there is still something missing in terms of *tikkun olam* (literally, *repairing the world*).

According to Elliot Dorff (2008), the concept of *Tikkun Olam* is a relatively new one, based on classical Judaism's terms of *hesed*, *tzedek*, and *mishpat*. Rabbi Dr. Dorff explains that *hesed* originally meant: *loyalty* – to God and to your neighbor. He further clarifies that *tzedek* means justice and that *mishpat* derives from the same root as *judge*, with the word *mishpat* expanding its meaning to *justice*. He concludes, "In the Bible the values of justice and kindness are often spoken of together to indicate that they balance and reinforce each other" (pp. 4-5).

How do you speak to yourself – with kindness and justice, or with harshness and judgment? These ways of thinking or talking to yourself may be the difference between feeling satisfied with life, or feeling lonely.

Tikkun Olam is an on-going and transformative process – it is never finished. Paulo Freire (2001) talked often of the *un-finished-ness* of our being, as well as of our being within the world, and of our identities in the process of ongoing (re)construction (pp. 52-62). He felt that "our teaching space is a text that has to be consistently read, interpreted, written and rewritten" (p. 89), and, as I would add, reinterpreted and acted upon. It is our incompleteness that opens up the space for both education and *Tikkun Olam*, which are entwined and which provide us with critical, reflective, liberating, and eternal hope.

Henry Giroux (2010) reiterates that "we live in a historic moment, both of crisis and possibility, one that presents educators, parents, artists, and others with the opportunity to take up the challenge of reimagining civic engagement and social transformation" (p. 76).

Maxine Greene (1988) elaborates on this difficulty, "We have been speaking of multiple perspectives, thinking about freedom in relation to community and to the possibility of a common world" (p. 87). A *common world* might be interpreted in many ways; I (Gail) see it as a common world of interconnected webs of positive relationships, repairing and bringing the world together.

As a community volunteer and activist, I frequently see this transformative power of working together for the common good, and in doing so we are able to identify the possibilities that lead to present and future hope, action, and love.

Telushkin (2000) adds, "We have a responsibility to make it clear to others what it is that we need. ...So don't just love your neighbor, make sure you give your neighbor a chance to love you" (p. 344).

Tikkun Olam is about being co-creators and co-repairers in a common world, in need of being constantly repaired. You are part of this co-creation, and that also means to co-create your relationship to loneliness.

The other day I (Harry) attended a reception for someone who had occupied a prominent position in our community and had been instrumental in getting things done. We had a conversation with one of the guests about the measure of a meaningful life. The honoree was a prime example of a successful life. She helped others find themselves after a period of deep suffering. She was instrumental in enabling others to also become prominent. The energy she introduced into other's lives triggered a whole new generation, giving new meaning to competence and prominence. In other words, our interactions affect other people. It is like a tickle – the whole body responds even though only one part of the body is targeted.

An example is the movie, *Schindler's List*. If you recall, at the end of the movie, many people came over to Oskar Schindler's grave to touch the stone. It was said that, because of his many intervening acts, 5,000 people are now alive. He was the creator of lives. If not for him, 5,000 individuals would never have been born, their parents' lives having been ended in a frenzy of shatter and destruction.

The Hebrew word for *death* is *maytim*. *Maytim* really means, *beings*. In other words, God's ultimate capacity is the reawakening of the dormant spark of life that still lives within it. God reignites and presents it with the possibility of continuing life on the planet or somewhere else.

In our Jewish tradition, we say that one of God's virtues is the ability to bring the dead back to life. This may seem silly, but is it really? What is life if not regeneration, being reborn, a new act of creation. Many of us in our older years are ready to close the book without realizing the ultimate future of our creations and our offspring. Many, in moments of despair, are literally ready to throw in the towel. In a very nonchalant way, I hear them say, "I've taken care of my children. It's now up to them. I've done my bit. Let them carry on," unwilling to affirm the continuation of generations.

How do we change our attitude so that we can see ourselves as progenitors of life?

First and foremost, we have to learn how to *number our days*. Every day has its moments of light and moments of darkness. In fact, the Bible tells us so: "And it was evening and it was morning one day." The sages have always felt that the evening is the darkness.

These sages came up with all sorts of rules and regulations about saying prayers in dark places, getting caught in dark places, what to avoid in dark places, as if to say there is an army of figures who are part of the darkness. Sometimes they were called *darkness*. Other times they were called *shaydim*. The Talmud is filled with various stories about *shaydim*, and we also find many stories about them in the Kabbalistic literature. At times they have been referred to as demons, and in the Jewish tradition they have had other names such as *Sheid, Mazzik, Ruach Hara, Se'it, Malach Mashchit* or any hosts of malevolent spirits that act "against humans beings, usually in the form of disease, illness, confusion, or misfortune" (Dennis, 2007, p. 65). You may know this phenomenon as the *evil eye* – poo, poo, poo!

Is *loneliness* the action
of one of these malevolent spirits?

In *Pirkei Avot*, also known as *The Ethics of the Fathers* (or Sages), we read, "Distance yourself from questionable neighbors." Some commentators said that this quote refers to the *shaydim*, always lurking in the dark places, hoping to snatch the innocent souls. If you can develop a counterfoil to the feelings of *shaydim present,* which so many have and possess, then do so. My (Harry's) father, *of blessed memory,* though skeptical of the power of *shaydim,* made sure "that the evil eye not befall us." The exercise of removing the power of the *shaydim* consisted of circling the *victim's* head with a handful of salt and reciting the formula, "I yearn for your protection, Oh God."

Many Jews believed, and still do, that this act will ward off the *evil eye,* the negative spirits that float around and park themselves on their chosen victims. The outcome of such choices may lead to a distortion of figures and unexplainable diseases. I can still hear some of my more traditional colleagues saying, "Don't be a *goy* (a nonbeliever)." Say the formula, i.e., *Zog kein ayin harah* – meaning, *May the evil eye not prevail.*

It is our belief in such forces that sometimes prevents us from acting on our own behalf. We have reached a point of understanding that the *shaydim* – like any of the other forces within or surrounding us– can be engaged in a discussion, which can turn them into a positive rather than into a negative force.

Some people pray to engage in positive ways. Telushkin (2000) explains that the Hebrew phrase, *to pray,* or *l'hitpallel* literally means *to judge and examine oneself.* Or better still, *to pray is to talk with oneself.* This meaning surprises many people since prayer is normally thought of as a petition, a coming before God asking for what we want. In fact, Jewish prayer books contain mostly communal prayers and praises. The definition of *l'hitpallel* clearly conveys what the primary goal of the prayer service is, "to motivate us to service" (p. 166); namely, the *service* of *repairing the world* – beginning with one's self.

In this chapter, we explored how loneliness might be the path to epiphany – to a state of clarity. That path might lead to the Jewish concepts of *tikkun olam, hesed, tzedek,* and *mishpat*. They might lead to *yetzer haTov,* or to *hitpallel*. Through this act you may attain a certain state of mind. The conversation is with yourself, negotiating towards a common ground.

Loneliness may be a human condition, but there are some ways to move beyond loneliness. And when doing that, one is not alone. In the next chapter, we will explore the similarities and differences between the experiences of loneliness and aloneness.

My peers, lately, have found
companionship through
means of intoxication
– it makes them sociable.
I, however, cannot force
myself to use drugs to cheat
on my loneliness
– it is all that I have
– and when the drugs and
alcohol dissipate, will be all
that my peers have as well.

– FRANZ KAFKA

Chapter IV

Loneliness vs. Aloneness

The thesis of the oneness of humankind is central in Jewish thought. God created the first human, and all humankind is descended from that one. Our thinkers and philosophers have always said that the world stands in need of repair. It never attained the level of unity that was the ultimate promise of the Creator.

In fact, every period of history seems to be riddled with competition, wars, and hatred. When tensions blow over, attempts at reconciliation are always made, but we always seem to fall short.

Our studies have shown us that this is true for every human. We enter this world with our hands clenched, as if we were ready to grasp whatever comes our way. When we leave, however, our hands are open as if it were all a pipe dream.

We have all heard the saying, "You can't take it with you. Spend it while you can. Live it up. Enjoy it to your heart's desire." This has led to a great gap between generations. If I am told, "Live it up. Enjoy yourself," I have a great excuse for not sharing. We recall the end of the second World War – when the United Jewish Appeal was formed – many of our fellow Jews said, "I've given enough. How much more can I give? What will be left for me?"

On the other hand, some Jews who realized that being a bridge between the past and the future was the reason for their survival during the horrible years of the twentieth century.

There were many plans afoot. What should the bridges be? What should the bridges do? Who will be the engineer and the designer? Who will be the fundraisers? Through the old game of hit and miss, leaders appeared, and Bridges were built.

And now that the bridges are built, too many of us, especially in our senior generation, feel that we did our part. Let somebody else take over. The guilt seems to be gone, and the urge for renewal has been silenced.

We would like to suggest that whenever we are in the process of renewing another person, we are also in the process of renewing ourselves. Like every great bridge, this process has a path going one way and another path going the other way. And the bridge is fully used once both paths are functioning.

I am alone when I am detached from the welfare of another. I am lonely when I seek that attachment. The one who lives alone will ultimately end up in the blank pages of an unprinted telephone book. The one who is lonely will at least be a footnote.

In the process of reaching out to another person, in an attempt to transcend loneliness, I am constructing a bridge of connection.

Some people have been able to create bridges that are superhighways, while others have put together rickety bridges ready to fall apart. How does one go about creating a bridge which merges aloneness with loneliness? This process involves four steps.

Step One:

If you reach the stage in life where you say there is nothing that you can do about anything, especially about relationships, then you are in the state of aloneness.

To overcome that stage, it would be best if you drew up a three-column list: the middle column, ALONE; the left-hand side, BECOMING; and the right-hand side, OVERCOMING. In the BECOMING column, list as best you can the factors that brought you to the state of aloneness. In the OVERCOMING column, list steps you have taken to move beyond aloneness. These can be for example: joining groups, finding friends, sharing life stories, and helping others. Thereby, we begin to see the factors which lead us toward aloneness as well as the steps which lead us beyond aloneness.

BECOMING	ALONE	OVERCOMING
Factors which lead you toward aloneness		Steps you took to move beyond aloneness
Staying inside all day	Staying away from people	Joining groups
		Finding friends
		Sharing life stories
		Helping others

Step Two:

Draw a line across all three columns. In the BECOM-ING column list in the order of power the moments or the processes that led you toward aloneness. In the OVERCOMING column, list those activities or programs that moved you beyond the state of aloneness.

BECOMING	ALONE	OVERCOMING
Factors which lead you toward aloneness		Steps which moved you beyond aloneness
Staying in house all day	Staying away from people	Joining groups
		Finding friends
		Sharing life stories
		Helping others
Processes that brought you toward aloneness		Activities that brought you out of aloneness
Negative thinking		Communal Prayer

Step Three:

Draw another line across all three columns. Now we come to the warning signals. In the BECOMING column, recall as best as you can the signals and hints leading you to believe that aloneness and isolation will become dominant unless confronted. In the OVERCOMING column, think back and list those thoughts and activities giving you hope and making you believe that you would not have to stay in a state of isolation.

There are times one may want to be alone. That is not a problem. We are addressing the loneliness within aloneness; a state which you did not choose; a situation for which no remedy has been initiated.

BECOMING	ALONE	OVERCOMING
Factors which lead you toward aloneness		Steps you took to move beyond aloneness
Staying inside all day	Staying away from people	Joining groups
		Finding friends
		Sharing life stories
		Helping others
Processes that brought you toward aloneness		Activities that brought you out of aloneness
Negative thinking		Communal Prayer
Warning signs		Hopeful signs
Didn't want to take a shower and be with people.		Attended a lecture with a friend. Felt energized and connected

No matter what, bear in mind that it was you who was initiating change. No special force was stepping in to bring order to your chaos. Nor did you rub a magical amulet suddenly producing a genie saying, "Yes, Master, your wish is my command."

Once you are convinced that you did it yourself, it will be possible for you to do it again and apply it to other areas that accentuate your aloneness. Above all, remember that you are both a giver and a receiver, even though at times it may seem as if there was more than one voice speaking within you.

You are the master of your fate. We begin with the belief that from the moment you left your mother's womb, you had within your arena of activity latent skills and latent possibilities, waiting to be acknowledged and waiting to be carried out.

Step Four:

When you have reached the point of extricating yourself from the cage of your aloneness, you will look about and ask yourself, "Where do I go now? My sense of aloneness has been with me most of my life. I feel like a prisoner who has just been released from confinement, and yet I lack the energy, force, and whatever is needed to move on." Since you had allowed the feeling of aloneness, now you must also allow yourself the feeling of going beyond.

Going beyond? What does that mean? There will be new feelings that you may not have previously experienced. These feelings may make you uncomfortable. Do not fight them. Allow yourself to experience them fully. You may have thought that the opposite of aloneness is a sense of fullness; and yet, within that fullness, you may experience confusion, indecision, joy, or even sorrow as well as aimlessness.

That does not mean these feelings are *bad* or even *inevitable*. It just means *they are.*

I (Gail) often work with clients who have a sense of overwhelming doom and loneliness that they do not want to face. Through the therapeutic process, I ask them to look directly at the thoughts and events that might be part of this cloud of doom. As they tell me of the different parts that make up this cloud of doom, they realize that it is fear itself that makes up a large part of the problem. By being able to look at the different (smaller) pieces, fear and doom subside, and people are able to act on and engage in those events that were previously immobilizing.

One way to approach this is with the *worry jar*, as we shall call it. Worry, like many emotions, can become habitual. Worry can exacerbate the feelings of loneliness and aloneness. I know many people who worry constantly throughout the day. I will ask them to write down all the things they worry about and put them into the *worry jar*. Added, however, is the clear instruction that they may worry for longer than only 15 minutes each day.

During those 15 minutes of worrying, they are to take out every piece of paper in the worry jar and devote all of their energy and attention to those worries for that time interval. At the end of 15 minutes, people often realize that nothing can be really done for many of their worries; surprisingly, however, they come up with ideas and ways to take action for solving particular issues of their other worries. The pieces of paper in the jar gradually become fewer, as does the time worrying and the time feeling alone or lonely.

Sometimes, people like to do this with a friend or a neighbor, learning about each other together. The concept of *Havurah* is a friendly foundational theme in Judaism, and *Hevruta* is a distinctively Jewish learning experience. *Havurah* literally means *company, society, group,* or *fellowship*. It refers to the recent movement among American Jews to form small, informal groups for prayer, study (Reimer, 1992), and celebration of Jewish holidays.

Heschel (1995) suggests that these extended family gatherings serve as a model for types of communal associations that transcend the nuclear family – a type of "voluntary extended family" (p. 25). Many people feel loneliness because they are actually alone – family lives far away, spouses have passed on, and old friends have moved away. A *Havurah* can create a new family structure. Once they no longer are in the state of aloneness, their loneliness will often lift as well.

In this chapter we linked aloneness to loneliness, and we set out ways and approaches to move beyond these. In the next chapter we will speak of loneliness not from the perspective of aloneness but from the standpoint of crowdedness.

I've also seen that
great men are often lonely.
This is understandable,
because they have built such
high standards for themselves
that they often feel alone.
But that same loneliness
is part of their ability
to create.

— Yousuf Karsh

Chapter V

THE SELF

– *I* VERSUS *WE* –

LONELINESS IN A CROWD

Loneliness in a crowd is a paradoxical experience. One would think that with so many people around, one would not feel lonely; however, sometimes the very act of being with other people magnifies the sense of loneliness when one is not in relationship with anyone else in the crowd. Lonely equals *one-ly*.

When you are in a state of *one-ly-ness*, that is loneliness. The Bible tells us that it is not good for an individual to live by him- or herself; therefore, "does a man leave his father and his mother and seek himself a mate." The truth of the matter is that loneliness is not a *physical* shortcoming. It is an *existential* shortcoming.

Many times, patients describe their dreams of being surrounded with images of institutions, buildings, traffic, and yet, they stand alone. Many times, their dreams will have people and things float through the air and pass right through them as they stand in the middle of the square.

Mahatma Ghandi, sitting and spinning, is never lonely. He is engaged by his action. Adolph Hitler is always lonely, never trusting even his closest allies. It all depends on the inner message and the inner choice. Are you alone? Are you by yourself? Or do you live in a community asking you to become involved? The choice is yours.

Many figures pass through us only when we stand detached, unrelated to anyone, not even being ourselves. We stand in judgment outside of ourselves judging ourselves. The psychiatrist and the psychologist call this a *neurosis*. We would like to suggest that it is not neurosis, it is simply being *unattached*. That is why the Bible says, it is not good for a human to live that way. That is not what God wanted.

Our sages, such as Hillel, and the Jewish Christian sage, Jesus, agreed in that "you shall love your neighbor as yourself," and this is the essence of our tradition. Hillel said to his inquirer, "now go study" – find out what the words mean. First and foremost, the verb translated as *love* in Hebrew is *Ahav*.

As you may recall, *Ahav* truly means *connectedness*. You and your neighbor, you and your God, you and yourself have a life task of bringing to the fore of your life, the oneness that is in essence *love*.

Buber (1996) also wrote of the *I–Thou* relationship as a deep reciprocal interpersonal connection, seeing the humanity and divinity within each person. *I–Thou* relationships are contrasted with *I–It* impersonal dealings. That is why Buber adds that since you love yourself with all your faults so you must "love your neighbor, no matter how many faults you see in him" (p. 83).

We might also add that for some people it is easier to love their neighbors, with all their faults, than it is to do the same for themselves. They might find it hard to love themselves, especially with all their faults. This can create deep feelings of loneliness. Yet, if one is obliged to "love your neighbor, no matter how many faults you see in him or her," the same *Ahav* treatment might also extend to oneself. This is where the potential power of *Ahav* resides.

The interesting thing is that loneliness and *Ahav* phenomena happen to most every human being. Yet, you may think that you are the only one who has ever experienced loneliness or experienced *Ahav*.

We are writing this book to present the universality of loneliness and to offer suggestions from one source of wisdom – our Judaism. Our Judaism grounds us in a communal setting. Most of our prayers are in the plural. We titled this chapter, *I versus We*, which really is a misnomer, since we do need both - the *I* and the *We* - in this process. They should not be in conflict with each other.

I (Harry) had a dream about being on vacation with my wife, and it was time to go home. I still felt that I had something to do, something to see, so I went looking for it. And of course I looked for that too long. And when I went back to look for my room, the room was gone. So was my wife. I went outside and stood in the square in front of the hotel, and I did not wear any clothes. And I wondered how I could get from one side of the street to the other. Maybe the answer is over there. Then I woke up.

What was the dream telling me? I was living an unconnected life. What was this business about deciding to leave my wife? Was I focusing on something else? Most of my life I have felt very separated, and I continue to seek the prime cause for this feeling. But wherever I turn, I feel that I am almost there, just not quite. And I am beginning to feel that to be the purpose of the senior years. And if you live a little longer than you anticipated, it might be due to the fact that you may not have finished your mission. Because what one person knows, all of us know. That was the basis Jung's teaching.

I (Gail), on the other hand, have lived, and continue to live, a very connected life. I do not share these *unconnected* dreams of Harry. My dreams are often framed in loving feelings and deep connections with other people, with nature, and with the ineffable. When I awake, I bring these feelings with me and to my interactions with the people I meet throughout the day – a sharing process that is a *tikkun olam* process – and one of many moments in which both the *I* and the *We* are joined.

In yet another one of Harry's dreams, an elderly person, scantily clad, was standing in the middle of a crosswalk, trying to figure out whether he should go east or west or north or south. There were labels on the clothes he wore; yet, he could not identify them. They were like notes stuck on a board, and he had forgotten why he placed them there. He stood for a few moments and then grasped all of his clothes – his shirt, his pants, whatever he could get a hold of – and he felt that this self-created bundle was the map that he was looking for. He smiled and continued walking on the sidewalk with a new sense of direction, a new feeling of purpose.

I (Harry) think all of us, at one point or another in our lives, have such moments. We think we know where we are going, and yet, the thread that ties everything together is invisible. We try to pray. We try to meditate. We try to focus. All is well and good. We sense the thread, but we only have a faint glimmer of it. When does the thread become distinct?

The senior days and the senior dreams can be an attempt to spell out the direction and the path upon which we are going.

Loneliness in a crowd is not knowing where to go. All the earmarks are there. The stores are lined up, the street signs are there, but we still do not know where we are. As if playing a Monopoly game, we cannot locate the properties. We own the properties, but we do not know how they fit together, and we do not know what to do with them.

This is the human condition. It is not that we lack the wisdom or the fuel or anything else needed in order to complete our journeys; but we lost a sense of connection. We do not know where to go, where to turn, what to think, what to feel, what to hope for. We try to act and stir the pot. We try to blend the ingredients, but we do not have either the moment or the skill that pulls everything together. Then our senior years come along, pointing all this out to us.

A better example is an individual who has just moved into a senior retirement center and wants to be part of the community. At first, he is given an ear. People listen to him. A judgment follows, and then he feels another door closing to him. God did provide you with your senior years to help you work through that puzzle, so that you can end at least with a smile on your face. You think you are getting somewhere. You sit down, they listen to you. Then, however, nothing follows. That is when your God-given gifts have to be brought into play.

Then the window opens, just like in the dream about the train in the subway mentioned in chapter 8. Whenever he opens the window, the train moves. Whenever he closes the window, the train stops again.

Your loneliness can only be broken by you. God gave you the opportunity to accomplish this. You have some extra years to come to terms with the erroneous steps you have taken in your lifetime. What can you do?

First, learn to forgive and forget. No erroneous act on your part lasts forever. Learn to forgive yourself, too. Follow these steps in the act of forgiving yourself: 1) Why did I do it? 2) Did I achieve any sense of relief for having done it? (Usually not.) 3) Having forgiven and forgotten, imagine yourself on a bridge that has collapsed. You wonder how you will cross the chasm. Suddenly, you see something floating in the water. You try to hold on to it. You try to paddle. And before you know it, you're on the other side.

When you are in the process of forgiving and forgetting, you fight it. How can I forgive? How can I forget? Somehow, somewhere, there is the hidden will that comes to the fore, and what you thought was never possible becomes very probable.

This does sound miraculous. And why not? What is a miracle but figuring out what could be done when you were convinced that any rectification was impossible? Some miracles occur without rhyme or reason; but most miracles are simply signs you picked up along the way which tell you how to get from one spot to another.

Have faith in yourself.
Have faith in your God.
Have faith in life.

Bear in mind that *loneliness*
often fuels *creativity*.

I (Harry) talk too much. I think too much. I argue too much – all of which is part of my creative process. I am always finding myself getting into a place of judgment. Sometimes I may not agree with people, or people will not agree with me; either I need to find my own community within the community, or I need to decide that I am enough. I need nobody else's approval, because the world, unfortunately, is full of people who have judgment in their hearts as opposed to love. I need to be the person with love in my heart for those with only judgment. Then I will be less lonely. I will have seen the divine spark within another individual. I can let go of judging their judgment. I can also tell them to kiss my derriere.

Maybe there should be a code for seniors, which reminds us of our third technique: humor. There are many books written about humor in general, and about Jewish humor in particular. All three of us rely on humor as part of mastering the loneliness paradox – we do that with humor directed at the "I" and with humor directed at the "We". Sometimes humor is the only tool at our disposal when we are suffering the throes of loneliness.

This chapter touched on some dreams and metaphors which capture moments of loneliness, individually and collectively. In the next chapter, we will further explore the theme of suffering.

Life is full of misery,
loneliness,
and suffering
– and it's all over
much too soon."

– WOODY ALLEN

Chapter VI

SUFFERING

There is a close relationship between Eastern thought and many parts of the Bible. If one reads Lamentations or Job or any of the other great philosophical works that appear in the writings of the Bible, one can sense a connection between Jewish and Eastern thought. This is because Judaism is an Eastern religion practiced in the West. All of Judaism's formative years were spent in the East. It became a "Western" religion only after the diaspora.

The Easterners always said suffering is an established fact (Armstrong, 2001). A.G. Johnson (2006), on the other hand, reminds us that "it is impossible to live in a world that generates so much injustice and suffering without being touched by it" (p. 63).

We Jews always say, "worry about what's troubling you when it happens, because it's part of the day. But don't think about it when it's not there." We who have reached the later years of our lives –by that I (Harry) mean beyond 75– will encounter more and more moments that reveal the not-so-good, the negative, the suffering moments of our lives.

Sit in a park or at any place where older people gather, and you will hear conversations that tell about the glories of the past, the achievements of children, and the missed opportunities; but seldom do you hear the greatness of the moment. As if to say, the worthiness of our lives is centered around things of the past. At a certain point in our lives, there is a break, and we find ourselves stuck. No movement. No creativity. No hope. Only despair.

Some of us find an energy stream within ourselves that speaks to us, "don't give up!" Most of us, when we receive this inner message, may respond: "What can I do? I'm too old. My glory days are gone. And all I see is a hazy future." Many of us caught up in this stream of thought join various groups in hopes of saving the day and halting the decline. Some succeed. Most do not.

If you visit retirement homes, you will find the same menu every other day and repetitious program events. The residents sit there with blank faces, and one wonders if the administration of the home is listening to their residents.

Our society seems to feel that past the age of the middle seventies, one cannot expect new creations, new ideas, new novelties. Recent studies by competent observers have said if you want the residents of these retirement homes to prolong their lives, then present them with meaningful moments. Humans were never created to live, generation after generation, in the same way. Change is the mark of the human. Change is the only constant.

It is interesting that we are talking about suffering. I (Gail) have observed many of my older clients being so focused on their past glories that they excluded present abilities and pleasures. As Harry talked about present moments – the *meaningful* present moments – I am reminded that people who constantly relive their pasts, have not only lost sight of meaningful present moments, but have created the perfect conditions necessary for incubating loneliness.

As part of my dissertation project, I combined older people's lifetimes of experiences with the ability to capture present pleasurable moments of service (volunteering) and connection that neutralized the loneliness. In my report I wrote,

> It turned out that the process of the Project was an enjoyable, relationship-laden, multi-perceptive, and caring exercise. The participants often mentioned feeling good about their service (helping others), their learning (making new connections to previous ideas and experiences), and their reflection (experiencing insights and change). They demonstrated these by their words, and their actions. They surprised themselves and each other in their abilities to transcend age and physicality. They shared questions never asked and thoughts never expressed. They liked being in a classroom setting that was vastly different from that of youth, listening to others while being heard, being part of something bigger than themselves, finding commonalities and appreciating differences, using the cognitive (dialoguing and reflecting) and the emotional (experiencing and caring)." (Bretan, 2013, p. 213)

People often confuse the terms pain and suffering. Pain is a universal experience, but suffering is a human-made condition. The ability to transform that suffering is also a human-made attribute. There is both pain and suffering in the feeling of loneliness, but these can be transformed by various means. In my studies and observations, I (Gail) have been delighted and amazed to see individuals make that transformation.

The possibility of transformation is open to everyone. Theodor Hertzel once said, *"Eem tirtsu, ayn zo agadah."* "If you will it, it's not a tale." We Jews always felt that if you have the right intention, then you can be assured of the desired results. In this case, if you wear the cement shoes of suffering, then their weight will bring you down.

Your thoughts, and your words – your inner language – can have a profound effect on your loneliness and your ability to transform it. According to Hudak & Kihn (2001), "Love and liberation from suffering both lie in a realm beyond language; they are directly experienced and immediate – not concepts" (p. 253). Yet others might say that nothing is beyond language – language is everything! Liberation from suffering is about the relationship and the understanding that comes from the connection between the liberating act of education and the relationships between people as they liberate each other. Therefore, as proof of the above statement, language (a system of signs) is formed in the "relationship" between signified and signifier. We call their relationship "meaning" (C. Bretan, 2014, personal correspondence).

Slattery (2006) describes in his postmodern theological proposal that diversity, eclecticism, and ecumenism bring us together to wisdom and justice. He claims that one must give everything away to become rich, let go in order to live, and experience suffering in order to understand joy (p. 103). That seems paradoxical. Must we experience the suffering of loneliness to experience fully the joy of connection?

Suffering has been a constant theme throughout Jewish history and collective memory. The annual retelling of the story of the Hebrew slaves at the Passover Seder is one such touchstone of suffering that was transformed, and has transformed generations. Shapiro (1999) comments that "the *Seder* becomes much more than a retelling of long-ago historical events. The purpose is clearly to interrogate our present world to find in it the current forms of enslavement and suffering, and to do that from the vantage point of hope and possibility about a world in which exile and injustice have ended" (p. 6).

The *Seder* is a teaching and learning opportunity in which we all are expected to communally participate and personally interpret the results within our present circumstances. Figuratively and literally moving from a slave existence and mentality, we can free ourselves from the enslavement that loneliness holds over us.

In this short chapter, we explored the human-made condition of suffering. In the next section, we will explore ways to transcend suffering and loneliness, two conditions which are often experienced together, and which feed off each other.

The best remedy
for those who are afraid,
lonely or unhappy
is to go outside,
somewhere
where they can be quiet,
alone with the heavens,
nature and God.
Because only then does one
feel that all is as it should be.

– ANNE FRANK

Chapter VII

TRANSCENDING LONELINESS

Often times in our older years, our loneliness becomes the context of a *suffering* program: *We're lonely, we suffer. We suffer, we're lonely.* And we never realize that one triggers the other. If you are stuck, do something about it. Do not stand there as if you had cement shoes. We stated that humans, as opposed to other animals, can transcend any situation including that of loneliness.

It is within a human's power to create new situations which overcome the unbearable suffering of loneliness, of emptiness, of futility, of days gone by, of days not fully lived, and of regrets. A wise observer once said, "Remove the pins and the dress will flow."

Carol, our cohort in crime, is a harpist. We noted that the harp is the loneliest-sounding instrument. When you pluck the strings, you get a hollow feeling behind the tone. That is called resonance. We all carry within ourselves different instruments. We are always pulling strings. We are always blowing hot air and bubbles (please pardon the mixed metaphor). We are always pounding, hoping for harmony.

We are looking for the moment when all the pieces will tie together, and a sense of the harmonic orchestra will appear. While you can play all the instruments individually, they are really meant to be played together. Often an individual will incessantly play his/her singular instrument and never explore and enjoy the beauty of the sounds of the other instruments as they are played together.

Transcendence occurs when we face the moment in which we find ourselves and say, *this is really not what I'm thinking*. Sometimes, behind the moment, within the moment, and around the moment, we sense something calling out to us. It is saying, "I'm here. Don't forget about me. Pay attention to what I'm saying. Include me, so that the tension of the moment will not act separately from me, but that it will penetrate into my deepest recesses and say, *Aha!*" Once that occurs, I am no longer the prisoner of the moment. I learned to accept the moment and shown the moment how it can be greater than its current self.

Each person needs to find his/her own way to this transcendence. Sometimes it can be found alone or through silence, like that *still, small* voice alluded to in the Bible. Sometimes it can be found in the company of others, in a loving presence, or even in an uncomfortable situation. Do not fear these moments. Welcome them, embrace them, make them your friends, and goose them into reality.

Many times in our later years, we suddenly feel that we missed the target. We have an insight that clearly shows us who we are and what we can still be. Some will shrug their shoulders and say, *it is too late.* Others, however, will say, *even when we are leaving this world, we were given the blessing of a bridge so that our departure will not be an empty gesture – the wonders will never end.*

Throughout the Bible, we have stories of people who felt they were at the end of their journey, but suddenly, something occurred, and they felt the need to admit that nothing ever ends. It may cease to be known, but it never ends. It is the shadow of which we speak, the possibility lying before us, the hope that our life has meaning. It is part and parcel of the guiding light that leads us from despair to hope and faith.

Our lives have been full of shadows, such as these. By churning and viewing the shadow, its negative hold dissipates. This is also the reason for utilizing the *worry jar*. It makes you take a look at those shadows and by doing so, it diminishes the shadow's perceived power over you.

I (Gail) once had a client whose life was full of shadows. He was experiencing severe physical pain. His doctor had pulled out his entire arsenal of treatments to try to help him. The doctor, in frustration, finally referred him for treatment to the pain management center where I was employed. In our assessment, we realized that this gentleman was severely depressed. He had recently retired, and shortly thereafter, his wife passed away. Unbeknownst to the doctor, he was now spending his entire day sitting in the middle of his living room staring at his four walls – no TV, no music, no company, no future. The shadows had overcome him. His loneliness and its ensuing suffering was all he had.

We immediately started psychotherapy and asked him to face his shadows. By doing so, he was able to identify that which was immobilizing him. He is now reconnected to the living world. He mentioned that the therapy had helped him transcend his physical pain, which was a manifestation of his psychic pain and suffering (loneliness). The fear of looking at the shadows was making him a shadow himself.

At times, we need to act, and to respond in ways that are dissimilar from the path onto which fear and loneliness direct us. Lerner (1994) emphasizes that the Torah asks us to respond to a different kind of voice – "a voice of love, justice, and transcendence" (p. 95).

Listen to that voice of love, justice, and transcendence! Love, *Ahav* in Hebrew, also means *connectedness*. Justice, *Tsedek (tzedek)* in Hebrew, means *making the crooked flat and even*. And transcendence means always realizing, no matter what we know and what we see, that there is something greater than what we see or perceive. If we can see our journey in life as the fulfillment of these three objectives –

a) making the crooked straight;

b) reconnecting so that all of us will be one;

c) realizing there is a protective cloud, always hovering over us, waiting to be discovered so that it may enter into our domain;

– then we can overcome those feelings of loneliness.

Life is a never-ending process. It has no beginning and no end. It always seeks another moment in which it can be understood in a deeper and greater way than previously achieved. That is why we say, as Jews, that everything is in a state of *becoming,* and seldom in a state of *has-been.*" Matter of fact, there is not *perfect tense* in Hebrew! If you were to ask a pious Jew, familiar with this transcendent God, "what did you achieve yesterday?" he will tell you, "I found the key to tomorrow."

We always had a song which reiterates that one should never see the road upon which one travels as the final road. Never say to yourself, *fini,* for the finish is only the beginning. In our journeys, individually and collectively, we remain *unfinished.*

The idea of *unfinishedness* is found not only in Judaism. Paolo Freire (2000) frequently writes about this state. When you realize that you and your fellow humans are *unfinished,* it is easier to shed the cloak of perfection, the vestments of pretension, the garments of grandiosity. You will allow yourself to welcome change and to embrace it as your friend.

Recently one of our dear friends lost his wife of 68 years. He came to me (Harry) in the throes of despair. He broke down, he cried, he said, "What shall I do? Up until now, when I woke in the morning, my wife was at my side. Who is there now?"

I said, "not her body, but her essence is still there. It will be with you, it will guide you, it will accompany you on all your journeys."

Our friend's wife passed away less than a month ago. He feels that he will help his wife's soul to find her resting place through the simple acts of helping others with whom he is engaged. He has rolled up his sleeves working as a day-to-day volunteer. A physician by profession, a guardian by commitment. This is the path he has chosen to ward off the shadow of loneliness. It is one of many paths.

A philosopher once said: *the mark of the Jew is the mystery of his continuous existence*. I think the fact we insist that there is no beginning or no end is the mark of our existence. It is a type of immortality.

This reminds us of a quote by Mark Twain (1897) about Jews.

> If the statistics are right, the Jews constitute but one quarter of one percent of the human race. It suggests a nebulous puff of star dust lost in the blaze of the Milky Way. Properly, the Jew ought hardly to be heard of, but he is heard of, has always been heard of. He is as prominent on the planet as any other people, and his importance is extravagantly out of proportion to the smallness of his bulk. His contributions to the world's list of great names in literature, science, art, music, finance, medicine and abstruse learning are also very out of proportion to the weakness of his numbers.

He has made a marvelous fight in this world in all ages; and has done it with his hands tied behind him. He could be vain of himself and be excused for it. The Egyptians, the Babylonians and the Persians rose, filled the planet with sound and splendor, then faded to dream-stuff and passed away; the Greeks and Romans followed and made a vast noise, and they were gone; other people have sprung up and held their torch high for a time but it burned out, and they sit in twilight now, and have vanished. The Jew saw them all, survived them all, and is now what he always was, exhibiting no decadence, no infirmities, of age, no weakening of his parts, no slowing of his energies, no dulling of his alert but aggressive mind. All things are mortal but the Jews; all other forces pass, but he remains. What is the secret of his immortality?

We are told that our patriarch, Jacob, was assured by our Creator that he need not fear. "Al Tira Avdi Yaakov." *Don't be afraid, Jacob my companion, the one who works with Me.* Do you remember the dream you dreamt and the message of the dream? No matter who stands up before you or challenges you, his form is never a final form.

I (Harry) am reminded of the poem by William Law:

The Deepest Part of Thy Soul

Though God be everywhere present,
    yet He is only present to thee
    in the deepest and most central part of thy soul.

Thy natural senses cannot possess God
    or unite thee to him; nay, thy inward faculties
    of understanding, will, and memory can only
    reach after God, but cannot be the place
    of His habitation in thee.

But there is a route or depth in thee
    from whence all these faculties come forth,
    as lines from a centre or as branches from
    the body of a tree.

This depth is the unity, the eternity, I had almost said
    the infinity of thy soul; for it is so infinite
    that nothing can satisfy it or give it any rest
    but the infinity of God. (p. 48)

In this chapter we touched on transcendence and *unfinishedness* as steps towards welcoming change and reconciling loneliness. Understanding that one is always in a state of flux provides perspective. In the next chapter we will see how relationships factor into these ideas of transcendence, unfinishedness, and change.

If you are afraid
of being lonely,
don't try to be right.

– Jules Renard

Chapter VIII

RELATIONSHIPS

Relationships are tricky. We want them, we don't want them. We yearn to be in them, and then when we are, we want to be out of them. We never seem to be satisfied.

We are the travelers on the train that passes by each station. Let me share a dream with you. A man was sitting in the Third Avenue L train in New York City. It had come up from the underground subway and now is elevated above ground. Whenever the occupant opens the window, the train moves. When he closes the window, the train stops.

Upon analysis, the individual in the train was the owner of the dream. And the story of the train was his story. Much of his life he had spent underground, in a subway, not knowing where he was going or what he was facing. He finally came above ground, but the train could only move if he engaged in the world around him.

How do you engage with the world around you?

Older people living in retirement homes will tell you various stories of engagement. Some –those who are assertive– see themselves as the pope and the leader, always on top of the crowd, always pontificating, always telling of the glories of their family, and always talking exclusively about themselves. Others are being passive, absorbing others' wisdom, and trying to make it their own. A third group retains its own integrity, not needing the judgment of others to assess the success or failure in their own lives. Where are you within this continuum?

If you are always telling others how they should live their lives, are you an expert on living yours? If you are always deferring to others judgment, will you ever truly start living your own life? Do you need a judge for your inner life telling you whether you passed or failed? Are you ready to stand up to those telling you that they know better, and will you quietly say to them: "I know my way. You know your way. Let's walk together."

In Judaism, the word *Halacha*, which we referenced previously, stands for an established corpus legally binding you to a text. The word comes from the Hebrew root *H-L-Kh*, which means to go, to walk, or to travel.

The traditional definition of *Halacha* is the corpus by which we Jews have lived for centuries – an accepted corpus, at times modified, but on the whole remaining intact. It is derived from the written and the oral law. I (Harry) believe that modifications can only come about by a highly regarded assembly of rabbis.

I (Harry) am suggesting a new definition. Instead of *Halacha*, which I see as a static process, I suggest we use the word *Halicha* to imply that concept of a journey. From my point of view, life is a *Halicha*, a constant, never-ending journey. Whatever I choose for myself to express my association with the group, my relationship to God, my understanding of myself and of others is forever becoming, becoming, becoming. It is a dynamic journey of self.

I (Gail) see *Halicha* as a hermeneutic (interpretive) journey that one takes based on the corpus but not necessarily limited by the interpretations of my predecessors. I see it as a living and evolving essence, entwined with my own life corpus, creating a new entity. I am the now part of the corpus, as are you. I see it as a connection – a journey we take together as the path unfolding before us.

If the senior can see him- or herself as in a constant state of becoming, then even the senior years are just another stage in the journey. Never final. Always becoming.

Our relationships travel on their own journey. The person I am today may not be the same person 20 years from now, or even 20 minutes from now.

Abraham Joshua Heschel once engaged a few students in the seminary hallway. One of them asked him a question. He gave an answer. The next day, at the same spot, Professor Heschel was encountered by a second student with the same question. Again, he gave an answer. But the student said that yesterday he had said something else. The professor answered, "That was yesterday. That is not today." We are ever in a state of becoming.

In chapter 5 we mentioned the *I–Thou* relationship (Buber, 1996) to be a deeply reciprocal, interpersonal connection which enables seeing the humanity and divinity within each person. The *I–It* relationship, on the other hand, is characterized by impersonal dealings.

Knowing that, you can choose to handle your relationships in a new or different manner than before. If your relationships tend to be one-sided or unfulfilling, you may choose to change how you react and interact with those around you.

In this chapter, we wrote of relationships and journeys. Both are constantly changing and *becoming*. Keeping this in mind, we will discuss ways to move forward in the next chapter.

Living the past
is a dull and lonely business;
looking back
strains the neck muscles,
causing you to bump into
people not going your way.

– Edna Ferber

Chapter IX

MOVING FORWARD

In previous chapters, we discussed the causes for our loneliness. We spoke of isolation. We spoke of ourselves versus the rest of the world. And we felt that all of these factors contributed to our loneliness. We would like to suggest a way out of this maze.

First, I (Harry) will cite the Jewish tradition of *Adam Karov L'Atzmo* (*man is close to himself*). A person can be either his own best friend or his own worst enemy. Many philosophers have said over the years that it all begins with the first human and it all ends with the first human, too. In a courtroom, we always say to the witness, "Do you swear the words you are about to utter to be the truth, the whole truth, and nothing but the truth?" We can only expect an honest answer from one who knows himself, feels responsible for himself, and is willing to testify whenever proceedings arise that include himself.

Therefore, if you want to go beyond the problems of loneliness, you have to come close to the problems which trigger the loneliness, namely, the sense of isolation so many of us experience in our later years, the sense of us versus the world. Often we act like King Midas, who owned most of the world, but was afraid to share his wealth and his knowledge with others.

He became a lonely figure in a world that could have been sumptuous and overladen with goods and gifts.

We said earlier that a human knows himself best. If we are willing to be truthful and truly want an answer to our loneliness, then we should articulate the causes of the loneliness.

I (Harry) have a friend who lives in a retirement community. His oldest child took it upon herself to help him feel at home in his new surroundings; but she erred when she acted as if she knew what was best for her elderly parent. She never bothered to discuss the situation with him. She would call in the morning, "Hello. How are you? I'm off to work. Good-bye." Despite the fact that father and daughter lived in close proximity to each other, psychologically speaking, they were worlds apart.

A busy father –one who is not present when the children need him– may end up in a situation similar to the one we are discussing: if Papa isn't around or if the children aren't around, the perfect family is more of a dream than a reality.

To get beyond the loneliness, you should re-establish the model of closeness from earlier years, or you should have parent and child look at each other in a different way. The two adult persons should engage in constant conversation about life's current problems and requirements.

Like two adults who work next to each other, they become aware of what is going on between them. Instead of having a relationship which says –whenever I need five bucks, I can always get it from my father–, create a relationship that is built on reciprocity and respect.

The older senior parent is trying, at this stage in his life, to move forward. His current friends are of his current world. The pieces of history he discusses with his current friends are of this moment.

For a rabbi or for any other executive to be effective, he/she must be of this world and not boast of symbolic moments, saying, "well, in my life, I'm of this symbol, I'm of this miracle, I'm of this special event," but rather, he/she must proclaim the possible outcome of current situations.

Now let us turn to the second point. Having established my authenticity, I can expect people to turn to me for conversation and possibly for advice. In recent years, when you would gather at a meeting of "important people," you would look for some story that casts some light on goings-on in the world today.

If we want to remain meaningful and effective, we have to prove to our audience that we are not stuck in our past. We have to strive for meaningful, relevant conversation. Staying relevant implies more than, "Let's talk about the weather. What did your doctor say?"

Speaking of the weather, during the recent severe storms, some of us became conscious of the scientific reviews that appear almost daily on the news stations. We would sit at the table, and someone would say, "I heard that the melting of the ice up north is very severe, and that we can expect floods throughout the North American continent."

At the same time, the Gulf Stream is acting up. And so you have the Gulf Stream and the Arctic air collide in the American Midwest. We talked about cities that were destroyed and cities uncovered as the snow and ice melted. One report even showed a frozen arm found in a mound of snow.

The conversation became very interesting with all sorts of people sharing bits of information. Then someone added, "every x-number of years, the same thing occurs; therefore, there is no need to feel this is Armageddon but rather a cycle of nature."

We know that in every cycle of nature lies the key to its future. In one of my books, I once stated, "In chaos, one finds the order for the next day."

My third point is once we have become engaged in discussions of the now, we can find the results of previous attempts to go forward. The recent floods in New Jersey are an example as are the persistent forest fires of the last couple of years.

Nature (God) has provided us with a means for solving our problems. In societies employing the experiences of older people for consultation, the sweetness of success is often tasted. Therefore, we are not left hanging by a thread, an illusion, or a carrot.

There are those among us who feel that nostalgia is the final answer. We say to ourselves, "if only we could go back to the days when we were young." Every so often, I slip into nostalgia, and I will tell –

whoever will listen– how my mother used to prepare for *Shabbat*. She made broad noodles for the *kugel* and thin noodles for the soup. She baked her own *challah* and went every Thursday to the local fish market to buy a fish for *Shabbos*. Her children would rebel against the smell of *gefilte fish*, but she made it anyway. She always prepared an entire chicken for the chicken soup.

As far as her *challah* was concerned, she would prepare the dough on Thursday evening, cover it, let it rise over night, and bake it on Friday.

I (Harry) have all these memories. Sometimes I wish I could go back to those days when things seemed orderly, sensible, and familiar, as I was surrounded by friends and relatives. But then I say to myself, disease and unemployment were rampant, and the comforts that we now have were unavailable to most of us back then. Nostalgia is only a wish, very seldom fulfilled. If we seek our peace in our senior years, the foundation of our house cannot be nostalgia but the reality of day-to-day living.

An example of illusionary memory is the movie, Amadeus. It begins with Salieri, Mozart's supposed competitor, who was forever jealous of him. He is depicted in his old age expressing his great resentment and bemoaning the terrible challenge posed by Mozart and his genius. Even at his old age, Salieri sought solutions to undermine Mozart's brilliance. The movie even ends with a dark figure representing Death, claiming his victory. Mozart never finished his most sacred work, his Requiem, and he died a pauper.

Many seniors attempt an inner reconciliation. They are forever bringing to mind moments of disappointment. Often when telling their stories, they embellish them with solutions and outcomes that never occurred. There is a saying in the Talmud, "A thought is not a deed."

We cannot be held responsible for our thoughts, only our deeds. The senior years must be a time of accepting our limits, our greatness, our weakness, of letting go of anything and anybody who rattles us from within the chambers of our own minds and hearts. The senior years are the years in which we try to arrive at our own peace of mind and not constantly respond to the threatening voices of our past lives. You have to let go, not only in the physical sense, but in the emotional and spiritual sense, too. We must put our peace above everything.

A few years ago I (Harry) had a dream. I was looking through a glass pane and saw a verdant field – a beautiful landscape, flowers here and there, little butterflies flying around, bees buzzing to one another, and a pond where large animals were bathing. I remember saying to myself in the dream, "At last I see the garden. Maybe now I'll find my peace." You may say the mind is not a faucet to be turned on and off; nor is it a raging river washing everything in its way. The raging river might be seen rather as evil that surrounds you and hate that swallows you. How can we achieve inner serenity when pain is lurking at the door of our consciousness?

Consider, though, that hatred has no power over the other parts of the dream. It may give you sleepless nights, ulcers, and acidity. It may prevent the peace that you seek in yourself from coming to the fore. But there still is that still small voice inside reminding you that nothing is to be gained from becoming the river's partner? Distance yourself from the raging river, and let it know that you do not seek revenge or vengeance; you only seek your own peace of mind. There is a higher presence within you. It is greater than the raging river.

If anything or anybody is wrong, do not grant them free rent. Do not let them continue to live within and around you. Do not give them a presence within your mind and within your heart. Let your mind and your heart harbor only those who are a source of your peace. The rest – let them go. In letting go of your hurt, you will live in peace. A peaceful you is a beautiful you. And soon it will say that *even this shall pass*.

At the moment you have the courage and the guts to say *No!* to the negative force pulling you away from yourself, you will be freed from the thorns and impediments that prevent you from being your true self.

In this chapter; we talked about moving forward. It is easy to get stuck in the past and to let it dictate your present and future life. However, we always have choices – and we may have discovered some new opportunities and strategies available to you. In the next chapter, the loneliness paradox …

Lonely people,
in talking to each other,
can make each other lonelier.

– LILLIAN HELLMAN

Chapter X

THE LONELINESS PARADOX

Why did we title this book THE LONELINESS PARADOX?

You can ascertain from this quote by Lillian Hellman that people often become stuck in patterns which do not serve their best interests. "Make friends" is a mantra often recited to lonely people, especially to older people who have lost loved ones, independence, and hope.

In gathering together with other lonely people who often focus on their losses, loneliness can be worsened and magnified. The paradox of loneliness resides within these pages and within each of us. This book explores this phenomenon and offers insight into contributing factors, as well as ways to transcend the loneliness. The loneliness paradox is not inevitable. It can be resolved.

When we (Harry speaking) were kids, we would hold a pin up on top of the *Chumash* (Bible). We would drop the pin, and the word where it landed was the guide for the day. We would calculate the value of the word based on the lessons of *Gematria*, which is sacred Jewish mathematics and numerology.

Thus, *Elohim*, Hebrew for *God*, equals one plus thirty plus five plus ten plus forty (1+30+5+10+40) – a total of 76. Seven plus six (7+6) equals thirteen, and thirteen (1+3) equals four, the perfect number. If the pin falls on that word, then we are being encouraged to continue with our thinking, for we are in the realm of perfection.

In the introduction of this book, we defined the Hebrew word for *elderly – zaken –* as an acronym for *zeh shekaneh hakhma,* which literally translates as *a person who has acquired wisdom.* In Gematria, *zaken* has the numeric value of 157. If you add these together (1+5+7), you get 13. If you add 13 together (1+3), you get 4. Four, as mentioned previously, is the complete number. A person is really a *zaken* when he or she has completed his or her life's mission.

What is the loneliness paradox? When you feel that your life's mission is complete in its *unfinishedness,* you might no longer feel a sense of loneliness. This loneliness can then be replaced with a sense of peace, of wholeness, of connectedness, of completeness.

We wish that for you and for all of us!

With *Ahav* (love),
Gail, Harry, and Carol

References & Suggestions for Further Reading

Armstrong, K. (2001). *Buddha.* New York, NY: Penguin Books.

Berlin, A., & Brettler, M. Z. (2004). *The Jewish Study Bible: Jewish Publication Society TANAKH* (trans). New York, NY: Oxford University Press.

Bretan, G. H. (2013). *Jewishly-Informed Mature Adult Service-Learning.* Dissertation retrieved from http://libres.uncg.edu.

Buber, M. (1996). *I and Thou.* (W. Kaufman, Trans.). New York, NY: Touchstone.

Dennis, G.W. (2007). *The Encyclopedia of Jewish Myth, Magic and Mysticism.* Woodbury, MN: Llewellyn Publications.

Dorff, E. N. with Wilson, C. (2008). *The Jewish Approach to Repairing the Word (Tikkun Olam): A brief introduction for Christians.* Woodstock, VT: Jewish Lights Publishing.

Foucault, M. (1975). *Discipline and Punish: the Birth of the Prison.* (A. Sheridan, trans.). New York, NY: Vintage.

Freire, P. (2001). *Pedagogy of Freedom. Ethics, Democracy, and Civic Courage.* New York, NY: Rowman & Littlefield Publishers, Inc.

Freire, P. (2000). *Pedagogy of the Oppressed.* New York, NY: Continuum International.

Giroux, H. (2010). *Politics after Hope: Obama and the Crisis of Youth, Race, and Democracy.* Boulder, CO: Paradigm Publishers.

Greene, M. (1988). *The Dialectic of Freedom.* New York, NY: Teachers College Press, Columbia

Harvard School of Public Health – MetLife Foundation Initiative on Retirement and Civic Engagement. (2004). *Reinventing Ageing: Baby Boomers and Civic Engagement.* Retrieved from http://www.servicelearning.org.

Heschel, A. J. (2005). *The Sabbath: Its Meaning for Modern Man.* New York, NY: Farrar, Straus, and Giroux.

Heschel, A. J. (1951). *Man is Not Alone: A philosophy of religion.* New York, NY: Noonday Press.

Heschel, A. J. (1983). *God in Search of Man: A philosophy of Judaism.* New York, NY: Farrar, Strauss, and Giroux.

Heschel, A. J. (1959). *Between God and Man, an Interpretation of Judaism.* (F. Rothschild, Ed.). New York, NY: The Free Press (Macmillan).

Heschel, S. (1995). *On Being a Jewish Feminist.* New York, NY: Schocken Books.

Jewish Publication Society. (1999). JPS Hebrew-English Tanakh: the traditional Hebrew text and the new JPS translation (2nd ed.). Philadelphia, PA: The Jewish Publication Society.

Johnson, A. G. (2006). *Privilege, Power, and Difference* (2nd ed.). Boston, MA: McGraw Hill.

Law, W. (1982/2003). God Makes the Rivers to Flow: Sacred Literature of the World (Eknath Easwaran, Ed.) Berkeley, CA: Nilgiri Press and Blue Mountain Center of Meditation.

Lerner, M. (1994). *Jewish Renewal.* New York, NY: G.P. Putnam's Sons.

Maimonides, M., ben Maimon, M., & Goodman, L.E. (Eds.). (1976). *Rambam: readings in the philosophy of Moses Maimonides* (Goodman, L. E., Trans.). New York, NY: Viking Press.

Sacks, J. (2005). *To Heal a Fractured World: The ethics of responsibility.* New York, NY: Schocken Books.

Sadler, W. A. (2006). Changing Life Options: Uncovering the riches of the third age. *LLI Review*, 111-20.

Safran, J. (ed.), (2003). *Psychoanalysis and Buddhism: An unfolding dialogue.* Boston, MA: Wisdom Publications.

Shapiro, H. S. (1989). *The Moral & Spiritual Crisis in Education: A curriculum for justice and compassion in education.* Critical Studies in Education Series. New York, NY: Bergin & Garvey Publishers, Inc.

Shapiro, H. S. (1999). *Strangers in the Land: Pedagogy, modernity, and Jewish identity*. (Studies in the Postmodern Theory of Education, 46). New York, NY: Peter Lang.

Shapiro, H. S. (2006). *Losing Heart: The moral and spiritual miseducation of America's children*. New York, NY: Lawrence Erlbaum Associates.

Shapiro, H. S. (2010). *Educating Youth for a World Beyond Violence: A pedagogy for peace: Education, politics and public Life*. New York, NY: Palgrave Macmillan.

Sky, H. Z. (2011). *A Jewish Dialectic*. Bolivar, MO: Quiet Waters Publications.

Sky, H. Z. (2008). *A Rabbi in Maine*. Bolivar, MO: Quiet Waters Publications.

Sky, H. Z., Trobisch, D. J. (2005). *Give Me Two Minutes of Your Time*. Bolivar, MO: Quiet Waters Publications.

Slattery, P. (2006). *Curriculum Development in a Postmodern era*. New York, NY: Taylor & Francis.

Telushkin, J. (1992). *Jewish Humor: What the best Jewish jokes say about the Jews*. New York, NY: William Morrow and Company.

Telushkin, J. (2000). *The Book of Jewish Values: A day-by-day guide to ethical living*. New York, NY: Bell Tower.

Twain, Mark. (1897). *On the Jews.* Quoted in *The National Jewish Post & Observer*, June 6, 1984

Glossary

Bashert. Yiddish word for *destiny or destined.*

Beliefs. The way we *think* the world is (not the way it should be).

Binary opposition. A conflict between two opposite poles, without consideration of gradations (such as big/small, liberal/conservative).

Brit. Hebrew word for *Covenant,* it often refers to circumcision of eight-day-old boys into the covenant of Abraham.

Challah. A special egg-bread, usually braided, that is served on Shabbat and festivals.

Concept. An organizing idea or mental construct in one or two words that categorizes a variety of examples. Concepts are timeless, universal, abstract and broad.

Corporeal. Having, consisting of, or relating to a physical or material body. Fleshy, not spiritual.

Covenant. In Hebrew – *Brit.* An ongoing relationship between God and the Jewish people, a sort of marriage, shaped by Jewish law or religious obligations/ service, prayer, and other spiritual actions such as *tikkun olam.* See also *Brit.*

Dialectic. Reasoning using dialogue as a method of intellectual investigation, it is the nature of logical argumentation or the juxtaposition/interaction of conflicting ideas and perceptions.

Duality. Having a dual nature. The theory of reducing the reality into two further irreducible opposing approaches – one is usually considered good and the other is not. Also see binary opposition, Cartesian Dualism.

Education. The concept and process of acquiring general knowledge via the theory and practice of teaching.

Ethics. The study of the moral value systems of right and wrong on human conduct and its consequences. It answers the question, "What is the 'good' way to act?"

Gemilut Hasadim. Hebrew phrase for *the giving of loving-kindness*. Also see *hesed*.

Halacha, Halakhah. The Hebrew word for *walking, path* or *to go*, it has come to mean *Jewish law,* both the written and oral traditions – and the *way* a person should walk or *go through life*. Also, *The Way*.

Halika. A dynamic journey.

Hahnasat Orhim. Hebrew phrase for *welcoming guests*, it has come to stand for the concept of *hospitality*.

Hashem. Hebrew for phrase literally translated as *The Name*, it is used as a substitute for writing or pronouncing the forbidden Y-H-V-H Tetragrammaton. (See also *Adonai* and *Elohim*).

Hasidic, Hasidism. Jewish religious and spiritual movement founded in mid-18th century in Poland by Rabbi Israel Baal Shem Tov (literally *master of the good name*), it is from the Hebrew word *hesed* meaning *loving-kindness* or *piety*. Hasid & Hasadim are followers of Hasidism.

Havurah. Hebrew word for *fellowship*, *group*, *society*, *company*, or *friendship*, it is also the popular contemporary American Jewish movement that forms small and informal groups for study, prayer, and holiday celebrations.

Heder. Hebrew word for *room*, implying *classroom*, it was a term used in the past for Jewish religious education, mostly for boys. In modern times, the term would stand for *Hebrew School*, *Sunday School*, or *Religious School*, and would include girls.

Hermeneutics. The Greek word for *interpreter*, it has come to mean the study of the theory and practice of interpretation.

Hesed. Literally the Hebrew word for *loyalty* to God and human, it has come to mean *loving-kindness*. It has also been translated as *grace* and as *love*.

Hevruta. From the Hebrew word for *friendship*, it has come to mean a Jewish interpretive social learning practice or hermeneutical conversation. Many people think of it as the Yeshiva style of two people learning together by interpreting and challenging the text and each other.

Hokhma. Hebrew word for *wisdom*.

Ineffable. Another name for God, this word means *indescribable*, which God is.

Juxtaposition: Placing side by side, especially for comparison or contrast.

Kabbalah. General term for Jewish mysticism, usually from the 12th century to the present.

Kashrut. Jewish dietary laws. Kosher.

Kavod. Hebrew word for *honor*.

K'hilah, Kehilla. Hebrew word for *community*, in the Diaspora it has come to mean a local Jewish community that provides for the needs of its members.

Kiddush. The traditional blessing and prayer recited over wine on Shabbat or festivals.

Maytim. Hebrew for *dead* (people), it can also be translated as *being*.

Mazel. Hebrew or Yiddish for *luck*, we also translate it as *constellation*. Plural form is *Mazalot*.

Mishnah. The second century rabbinic legal code that forms the basis of the *Talmud*, it is divided into six parts, or orders, which are organized by topic into sixty-three short books, known as tractates.

Mishpat. Hebrew word for *legal precedent,* it has come to mean *rules* or *justice.* The plural is *Mishpatim* which has come to mean *rules* or *obligations.*

Mitzvah. Hebrew word for *commandment* from God, it is also commonly used to denote a *good deed*. There are 613 commandments in the Torah; the best known are the *Ten Commandments*.

Moral. Principles, guides, and ideas that focus on the ways in which human beings relate to other human beings and to the world, usually in terms of good versus bad behavior or character.

Mussar. A form of Jewish ethical living and practice.

Neshama. Hebrew word for *soul* or *breath*.

Oxymoron. A combination of contradictory or incongruous words (such as jumbo shrimp), or a concept that is made up of incompatible elements.

Philosophy. Literally the Greek word for *lover of wisdom*, it is what people do when they try to understand central truths about themselves, and the relationship of these truths to the world and to each other. It is asking and answering life's most basic questions.

Pirkei Avot. Usually translated from Hebrew as *Ethics of our Fathers*, it is the best-known book of the *Mishnah*, containing favorite maxims and teachings of many generations of different rabbis. I translate it as *Ethics of our Ancestors*, even though the teachings are exclusively by men. I have also heard it translated as *Ethics of our Sages*.

Principles. A generalized tenet that holds consistently over time, it is an accepted or acknowledged rule of action or behavior.

Process. The undertaking of a series of (systematic) actions or steps linked together to accomplish a specific goal.

Rabbi. Hebrew word for *My Teacher*, it was first used in the first century CE to describe someone who is committed to living and teaching the Jewish tradition. In contemporary times, it refers to Jewish ordination or clergy.

Rahamim / Rahmanut. Hebrew word for *compassion* or *compassionate*.

Reflection. Evaluating the assumptions upon which our beliefs and values have been assembled that shape our thoughts and actions.

Rosh Hashanah. The beginning of the Jewish year, it is one of the High Holidays (*Holy Days*) that occur in the fall.

Seder. The service at Passover holiday celebration.

Shabbat. The Hebrew word for *Sabbath*, it is a day of rest on the seventh day of the week (in Judaism from Friday night to Saturday night).

Shaydim. Dark Forces that reside in the deepest recesses of our mind.

Shekhinah. Hebrew word for *indwelling*, it is the divine presence in the world. In Kabbalah, the *Shekhinah* is the feminine aspect of God.

Shema. Hebrew word for *hear* or *listen*, it refers to the Biblical verse beginning with the word *Shema* found in Deuteronomy 6:4.

Shiva. The traditional seven days of morning after the death of a loved one.

Shoah. Hebrew word for *catastrophe*, it is also called the *Holocaust* because of the catastrophic destruction of European Jewry during World War II by the Nazis.

Shofar. The ram's horn generally blown during the Jewish High Holidays of Rosh Hashanah and Yom Kippur.

Siddur. Hebrew word for *order*, it refers to the Sabbath and daily Jewish prayer book that follow a certain order and structure.

Sim__ha. Hebrew word for *joy*.

Sitra Achra. Hebrew for *the other way*.

Tallit. Jewish prayer shawl.

Talmud. From the Hebrew root for *study,* this is the central text of rabbinic Judaism that was compiled at the end of the sixth century. It consists of the *Mishnah* and *Gemara* (commentary on the *Mishnah*), including both, *halakha* and *aggadah,* and using the same pagination (see Chapter III). It usually refers to the Babylonian *Talmud*, not the *Yerushalmi* (Jerusalem) version.

TaNaKh. An acronym for the Jewish Bible, it consists of the **T**orah (the five books of Moses), **Na***vi'im* (prophets), and **K***etuvim* (writings).

Teshuvah. Hebrew word for *re-turning* or *returning*, it has also come to mean *repentance*.

Theory. The speculation that explains an observed phenomenon, it can also mean an ideal or proposed set of principles.

Tikkun Olam. Hebrew phrase for *repairing the world*, it has come to characterize Jewish social action.

Tikvah. Hebrew word for *hope*.

Torah. Hebrew word for *teaching, instruction,* or *direction,* it can refer to the *Five Books of Moses,* the *scroll* that contains the *Five Books of Moses,* the *oral law,* and/ or all of Jewish instruction. Christians refer to it as the *Old Testament.*

Tzaddik, Tsaddik. From the Hebrew word for *justice (tzedek),* it has come to mean a *righteous* or *pious* person. Also used for the leader of a *Hasidic* community.

Tzedek. Tzedakah. Hebrew word for *justice* or *righteousness,* it also has come to mean *charity.*

Values. The principles we live and make judgments by, it is formed by what we think, believe, and do that is good, virtuous, and well-meaning. It is how we believe the world *should* be.

Yeshivah, yeshivot. Traditional Jewish academy for study of Jewish sacred texts.

Yetzer haRah. Hebrew for *questionable (or bad) inclinations.*

Yetzer haTov. Hebrew for worthy (or good) inclinations.

Yiddish. The Jewish-German hybrid language that has been spoken by Ashkenazi Jews from eastern and central Europe since the Middle Ages.

Yom Kippur. Jewish *Day of Atonement*, it is a solemn day for fasting and repentance.

Zaken. Hebrew word for *elder*.